SCARED:
GROWING UP
IN AMERICA

AND WHAT THE EXPERTS SAY
PARENTS CAN DO ABOUT IT

GEORGE H. GALLUP
WITH **Wendy Plump**

MOREHOUSE PUBLISHING

Library of Congress Cataloging-in-Publication Data

Gallup, George, 1930-
    [Growing up scared in America]
    Scared: growing up in America : and what the experts say
parents can do about it / George H. Gallup, Jr., with Wendy Plump.
        p.   cm.
    Originally published: Growing up scared in America. Princeton :
George H. Gallup International Institute, 1995.
    Includes bibliographical references.
    ISBN 0-8192-1662-3 (paper)

    1. Teenagers—United States—Social conditions. 2. Teenagers—
United States—Social conditions—Statistics. 3. Teenagers—Health and
hygiene—United States. 4. Teenagers—Health and hygiene—United
States—Statistics. 5. Social surveys—United States.
I. Plump, Wendy. II. Title.
HQ796.G325 1996
305.23'5'0973—dc20

                                          96-3210
                                          CIP

About the Surveys

The surveys among teens on which this book is based were conducted by The Gallup Youth Survey, a division of The George H. Gallup International Institute.

The Gallup Youth Surveys, directed by Robert Bezilla, are based on nationally representative samples of at least 500 teens, ages 13 to 17, and are conducted throughout the year by telephone. The results are released by the Associated Press Newsfeatures and are subsequently reported in YOUTHviews, the newsletter of The Gallup Youth Survey.

Readers are cautioned that these survey results, as are results from all sample surveys, are subject to "sampling error," a statistical estimate of the extent to which the survey results might differ from those that would be obtained had we interviewed all teens. Most of the survey results reported in this book are based on a sample of 500 teens, and results can be expected to vary by no more than plus or minus six percentage points. Results related to smoking, drawn from a survey funded in part by The Robert Wood Johnson Foundation, are based on a sample of 1,000 teens with sampling error of no more than plus or minus three percentage points. Results related to suicide, funded in part by Empire Blue Cross and Blue Shield, are based on a sample of 1,600 teens with sampling error of no more than plus or minus two percentage points.

Introduction
George H. Gallup

Children growing up scared in America? It seems hard to imagine in what we like to believe is an enlightened nation with vast human resources. Yet if the quality of life in a country is directly related to the well-being of its children, then our nation in some respects is not meeting this test very well.

The sad fact is that many young people across the land, in homes of both the privileged and underprivileged, worry daily about their physical well-being — not only on the streets of towns and cities, but at school, and even at home. They are apprehensive about the future, and a host of problems relatively new upon the scene: the threat of AIDS, the availability of potentially deadly drugs, and random death and violence, just to name a few.

Gone for many are key support systems that in the past were important to child-rearing and a young person's sense of security: strong families (torn apart today by the epidemic of divorce and other forces); friendly and supportive neighborhoods; and a society generally in agreement on vital core values. It is little wonder that many adults today are glad they are not growing up in today's world.

The Gallup Youth Survey over the last two decades has regularly interviewed young people to explore in depth their behaviors and attitudes, separating fact from impression or hearsay, to provide a reality check. Here is an overview of what we have found:

In cities and suburbs alike, America's teens are meeting violence in their schools and in their homes...The twin threats of unwanted pregnancies and AIDS make teen sexuality more complicated — and more dangerous — than ever...Bad eating habits, poor attitudes toward exercise and too much fatty food combine to make America's teens among the least healthy of developed nations...Drug and alcohol abuse, pervasive among teens in this country, are linked not only with higher juvenile crime but with higher rates of teen suicide...Too many American teens lack the one weapon they need to confront the risks they face — solid values, rooted for many in religious faith.

Young people caught up in risk behaviors are unlikely to attain the levels of education required for survival and success in a world that is growing increasingly complex and competitive. And school failure too often leads to chronic lives of crime, unemployment, or welfare dependency.

Each chapter in this book both describes and prescribes. First we show what our surveys among teen-agers tell us about each kind of risk behavior, whom it affects and the underlying forces. We go directly to young people themselves, so this book is based on reality, not simply theories on what people think is occurring among youth today. Next we report the advice of leading authorities we gained through interviews granted especially for this book on how to deal with each of these risk behaviors or problems. These authorities represent many fields, including education, suicide prevention, family violence prevention, drug abuse prevention, religion, character development, health and physical fitness, and child abuse prevention.

The steps set forth by experts at the end of each chapter are designed to help you deal with difficult situations. But it is important, of course, to remember that such steps should always be undertaken in the context of sound parenting principles, such as being firm but fair, and willing to listen to young people and their hopes and fears. Think of the good that could come in society by the simple act of parents spending even just a few minutes with a child each night at dinner or bedtime, asking the question, "How did things go today?" and then listening, followed by a hug, and three words: "I love you." Many would add prayers and reminders to children that they are loved by God.

One cannot exaggerate the importance of paying close attention to the spiritual life in raising children. In American society, in which the vast majority of people believe in a transcendent God who participates actively in lives and can be reached by prayer, many parents and others believe that the best way to help children avoid risk behaviors and to prepare them for the challenges of life is to encourage them to center their lives in faith in a living and loving God.

The benefits of such a faith are well-documented by surveys. Youngsters with a sincere and healthy faith dimension to their lives tend to be happier and better adjusted to life than their counterparts, as well as more likely to do well in school, and more apt to keep out of trouble.

Furthermore, a Gallup study for the Robert Schuller Ministries suggested that the nearer one feels to God, the better one feels about oneself and others. This is a highly significant finding from the point of view of our society, because the same study shows that as many as one-third of the populace have a low sense of self-worth, and such negative feelings about oneself are known to relate to a wide range of anti-social behaviors.

Those parents and others who place importance on faith development in traditional terms should be encouraged to lead their young charges to reflect upon, and eventually come to terms with, those basic questions that can determine the course of one's life: Who is in charge of my destiny — is God, or am I? To what extent is God the central motivating factor in my life? Are the basic rules of life given by God or made by humans?

At times it is important that a parent or concerned adult intervene directly in a young person's life — firmly but with love and compassion — if a risk behavior is involved.

In the back of this book, the reader will find vital resources for helping young people (perhaps your own child or children): crisis hotlines, and health, education and youth advocacy organizations. In addition, a listing can be found of publications recommended by the experts consulted for this book.

A final word: Much of the survey information presented in this book is about discouraging trends among youth in America today. And there may, indeed, be good reason to believe that young people today in some respects have it worse than their parents, but the prospects may not be all that bleak. The Gallup Youth Surveys also underscore the compelling qualities of youth — their idealism, optimism, spontaneity, and exuberance. Young people tell us they are enthusiastic about helping others; willing to work for world peace and a healthy world; and that they feel positive about their schools and even more positive about their teachers.

In our Gallup Youth Surveys, large majorities of American youth report that they are happy and excited about the future, feel very close to their families, say that they are likely to marry, want to have children, are satisfied with their personal lives, and desire to reach the top of their chosen careers.

But youth are threatened on all sides. Much good is at stake, so let us as parents, guardians and concerned adults commit ourselves to do everything we possibly can to help today's young people — tomorrow's parents, citizens and leaders — avoid or overcome risk behaviors, so that they can move forward into the future with greater hope and confidence.

Table Of Contents

CHAPTER 1

Home and School — Not So Safe Havens

REALITY: In cities and suburbs alike, more of America's teens are meeting violence not only on the streets but also in their schools and in their homes.

T wo of the most common and troubling misconceptions about violence in our society today are that violence is largely limited to the mean streets of urban areas, and that teens experience more violence from television and movies than from any other source.

This is simply not what America's teens are saying. They experience violence in an all too personal way and in environments frequently thought of as havens of safety and stability: their schools and their homes. Surprised? Here is one example of what can happen in "safe" suburbs.

At least one mother in an upscale suburban New York community thought something was amiss in the phone calls her 13-year-old son received one evening. The conversations were broken and whispered. Each call was followed by another in rapid succession.

Later that night the mother questioned her son, an eighth-grader at the Shoreham-Wading River Middle

School in Long Island, about the phone calls. The boy told her that he had been discussing soccer practice with some teammates. He was lying.

The next day, the mother received an urgent phone call from the school asking her to come to an emergency meeting. It was only then that she learned her son had been one among many who brought weapons to school that morning — baseball bats, crowbars, nickels wrapped in tape, a B-B gun, an air pistol. In an incident that would eventually implicate some 70 eighth-grade students, three young boys had planned a riot directed against students from a neighboring school district. They were fighting over an eighth-grade girl, over traded insults, and over the idea that loyalty among friends is something you don't question.

REGULARLY FEAR FOR THEIR PHYSICAL SAFETY AT SCHOOL	
1977	18%
1985	21%
1992	24%
1994	25%

Scores of newspaper stories detail how similar incidents came to disastrous ends in the death of a child, the injury of fellow students, the loss of innocence for a whole school community. In this case, the incident ended without injury — the weapons were noticed and confiscated as kids boarded afternoon buses, and school officials responded immediately. But it shook the district to its core. How could children in such a good school, one lauded nationally for its achievements, have gone so wrong?

Ross M. Burkhardt, President of the National Middle School Association and a teacher at Shoreham-Wading River, gives the only answer he feels is fair: "Others think this is not going to happen in their districts. It can and eventually, it will."

Mr. Burkhardt's prognosis is sadly on-target. To prove it, here are some of the statistics we've gathered from teen-agers on violence in the schools.

Violence in Our Hallways

Among the most alarming reports, 28% of teens say they are aware of peers who have carried or regularly carry guns and knives when they are in school. In fact, some 21% of teens had a best friend who was attacked within the past year by someone wielding a lethal weapon.

Some 69% of teens say classroom disturbances are a fairly large concern day in and day out. Another 58% say fighting in the schools is a problem. And 28% agree that the problem of weapons in the schools is an issue.

One teen in four says there was at least one time in the past 12 months when they feared for their physical safety while in school classrooms or hallways, on playgrounds, or walking to and from school.

One student in 10 had been hit by a teacher or a principal within the past

WEAPONS IN SCHOOL	
Aware of peers with guns and knives in school	**28%**
Believe weapons in the school are a problem	**28%**
Best friend attacked by someone carrying a lethal weapon	**21%**

year. Although this is bad enough, teens report that they are most often their own worst enemies. Peers, it turns out, are the biggest source of violence against each other. Half of the teens we surveyed say either they or a best friend had been beaten by someone their own age, while another four in 10 say they had been bullied by an older teen-ager. And in a burst of candor, some 12% of teens say they themselves had inflicted harm on someone within a school environment.

Vandalism and theft also have an all-too-common presence in our schools. Some 15% of the teens we surveyed report that they had something of theirs stolen. Another 14% had their property vandalized at school.

It is important to stress that our Youth Surveys target teen-agers from all walks of life, from all regions, from all types of environments, urban to remote and rural. It is not as if the most discouraging statistics were drawn from embattled urban districts and neighborhoods. In fact, as the case with Shoreham-Wading River bitterly proves, they reflect all too accurately what is going on in every district and community throughout the country.

> *"Even the hardened physician cries when he sees adolescents die prematurely."*

For example, one 17-year-old young man from an upscale suburban high school told us, "I knew a kid in eighth grade who brought his father's gun into school to show it off, and kept it in his locker for like three days. I thought it was pretty cool then. But now I think about how easily something could have happened, and how he acted for those days —so tough and loud-mouthed — and I can't believe nothing did."

Need for Action Well-Documented

What can be done about violence in the schools? Certainly the spotlights of media publicity have underscored how much at risk teens are in their school environments. At the same time, the focus has been more on sensation and less on solution.

This fact has brought many organizations that deal with adolescents to their knees in a very public way, pleading with Americans to do something about the scourge of teen violence. One such organization is the American Medical Association. So concerned is the AMA with the realities its members face every day that President Dr. Robert McAfee has made fighting violence — and not health care reform — the centerpiece of his tenure. During his interview with us, he discussed this commitment and its origins:

"Even the hardened physician who sees and deals with the consequences of violence day in and day out cries the most when he sees adolescents die prematurely," says Dr. McAfee.

"If you know how hard we struggle to extend lives at the other end of the scale, where we can get maybe two or three years added to an elderly person's life, then to see a 20-year-old's life cut short by a bullet and lose 50 years of life, you begin to say, 'Why am I doing so much at the other end of the scale when I'm not focusing on this end?'"

During a lengthy discussion on how parents can help halt violence in the schools, Kathryn Whitfill, President of the National Parents and Teachers Association, says parent-school partnerships are essential. Rather than lose perspective in the face of overwhelming societal problems, Mrs. Whitfill urges parents to "jump in with small steps."

Small Steps for Change

Many parents these days are patrolling school hallways before and after school hours, says Mrs. Whitfill. Some have formed groups of neighborhood kids and walk them back and forth to school, taking turns with other parents. Many communities have Safe Houses programs in place, in which children know through a printed poster in the window or a front-door decal that they can duck into a house if they feel threatened while walking to and from school. Nearly every local PTA, says Mrs. Whitfill, can assist parents with setting up such programs. Some even have in-depth training available for parents.

One of the biggest concerns parents have when their children leave the home each morning is who their child will be spending time with all day. Mrs. Whitfill insists that parents have a right to know who their kids' friends are. The best way to find out? Ask. Invite their friends over to your home. Get to know them. They have a lot of influence on your child.

> *"You can't protect them forever, but you can keep them from walking into a buzz saw."*

And if your children are going to a party somewhere, she says, don't hesitate to find out everything you need to know for your peace of mind — even at the risk of embarrassing your teen-ager. "Parents must know that they have a right to sit down and say, 'If you're going to this party, I want to know who you are going to be with, and when you are going to be home. I'm going to call the parents and make sure they'll be there supervising.' Now as you know, this is embarrassing as the dickens to a lot of kids.

"Nevertheless, I don't think it's out of line for a parent to do that," says Mrs. Whitfill. "They feel it's interfering in their child's life. It's not. It's really just protecting their child's life. You can't protect them forever, but you can keep them from walking into a buzz saw."

One route to involvement that can never be overemphasized, she adds, is also one of the easiest steps for parents to take: Write a letter to the teen's teacher or principal. Let them know where you are during the day so you can be contacted if there is an emergency; tell them you want to know if your child is doing particularly well — or poorly; tell them to call you if your child is causing trouble in the school.

Insist on being involved. Parental intervention, says Mrs. Whitfill, is perhaps the most potent force in thwarting violence in the schools.

"My approach is this: You can do something about what's going on in your child's life," says Mrs. Whitfill. "You need to just take one small step, and then things will build from there."

Better Student-Teacher Relationships

National Middle School Association President Burkhardt is unequivocal about the elements that brought about a peaceful conclusion to the would-be riot of 13-year-olds at his school. For one thing, he says, teacher-student advisory groups are absolutely essential. These involve small groups of teens — 10 to 12 — assigned to every teacher in the school. They meet at least once a day, usually during homeroom.

"You can do something... You need to just take one small step."

They talk about all sorts of subjects ... current events, school events, personal concerns. And several times a year, teachers are required to meet individually with each advisee.

"I, for instance, am required to have seven conferences a year with each of my advisees," says Mr. Burkhardt. "Just to say, is there a problem in your life? Let's talk about it. So kids genuinely feel they are listened to and they are known. And that anonymity that exists in many school settings does not exist in our school."

The advisory group became the focus of much necessary discussion in the wake of the discovery of the riot plans. If there aren't any such programs in your teen's school, why not work hard to get one started?

Mr. Burkhardt also points to the school curriculum, which he says must be student-driven. Biology, math, reading are important, absolutely. But in some cases schools need to be willing to "throw the regular curriculum out the window" when an emergency arises, and turn its implications into a learning opportunity. Teachers at Shoreham-Wading River did just that after the riot plan discovery. For two days they focused almost exclusively on the larger questions surrounding the incident: What is loyalty? What price friendship? What should you have done? What would you do next time? In short, they talked things out and took as much time as they needed.

A few days later, when Mr. Burkhardt's Social Studies classes returned once more to the regular curriculum — which just happened to include the Cold War — Mr. Burkhardt said he would be drawing some connections between the past and the present. "I'll be bringing in the issue that wars boil down to something somebody said, and issues of pride, and issues of understanding." It's a case of making the curriculum "real" for the students. And it makes all the difference.

Home — a Source of Rage

We shift the focus now to the home environment, which these experts believe could be the single most significant factor in the origins of violence. Teens had something to say about that, as well. For starters, nearly half of the teens surveyed, some 46%, say there are guns in their homes. This represents a slight decrease from 1985, in which 55% of teens said there were guns in their homes.

One teen in four has a friend who has been hit or physically harmed by a parent in the past year. Some 26% say they themselves have been hit or harmed by a parent or by another adult in the household. And this does not include verbal or psychological violence.

Half of the teens surveyed, 51%, say there is more crime in their home areas than there was one short year ago. And four out of 10 teens — usually thought of as adventurous — say they live near at least one area in which they would not walk alone at night.

Nearly half of all teens say there are guns in their homes.

While 59% of teens say they worry about teens imitating the violence they see at home on television, only 18% say their parents are "very" strict about what they are permitted to watch. About the same number, 21%, say their parents are "somewhat" strict about prohibiting them from watching violence on television. This leaves an enormous, alarming middle ground of "it's OK."

At the same time, 68% of teens think parents exaggerate the significance of violence in such shows as the MTV network's "Beavis and Butthead" cartoon. The same percentage of teens simply does not feel that there is too much violence in Saturday morning cartoons.

So how are kids at risk for violence in their homes? Where are they experiencing it? It apparently comes in all forms, including those that few parents recognize. That is the bleak message Dr. Richard Gelles, Director of the University of Rhode Island Family Violence Research Program, tries to drive home each time he confronts the fall-out of family violence.

Violence Is Manifest in Many Forms

"The public is pretty much convinced," says Dr. Gelles, "that family violence is something where you have to be laid out in a coffin or have photographs with bruises and cuts all over you, and everything below that is somehow OK.

"Especially around the issue of adolescent violence. If you whack a kid in the mouth with your fist because they've sworn at you, there's a position among parents that

PHYSICAL VIOLENCE AT HOME AND SCHOOL	
Have been hit by a teacher or principal	10%
Have been hit by a parent	26%
Recently were hit or had a best friend who was hit by a peer	49%

says that's OK because that's discipline. We take the position that it's still a violent act. You can call it whatever you want, but it's family violence."

This is a difficult message for most parents to digest. Accustomed to recognizing problems outside their own families, parents nevertheless hesitate to turn a harsh spotlight on their own practices. This is understandable, says Dr. Gelles, as everyone wants to assume they are parenting successfully. But a little serious, objective self-scrutiny never hurts. And it may even uncover some serious and problematic behavior.

"Hitting or abusing teens physically is fairly obvious family violence," says Dr. Gelles. But, he says, so is swearing at teens, humiliating them, screaming at them, verbally abusing them, and destroying their property. Some parents use passive aggression so effectively that they're not even aware of it — but the teen is always aware of it, he says. Examples include the silent treatment, ignoring children, shunning teens, or banishing them unnecessarily to their rooms and prohibiting them from having a role in the family.

"Half of all teen-agers' parents are still hitting them and yelling at them" when they finally enter their teens, says Dr. Gelles. Often the outcome of all of this at the other end is drug and alcohol addictions, as well as escalating forms of crime.

Dr. McAfee of the AMA takes the position that the most valuable dollars spent on preventing teen violence are those spent on children under the age of six. Six? Yes, says Dr. McAfee. "No doubt about it. Because, you see, by the time you get to school, you've already decided how you're going to solve conflicts. The violence you see between your father and mother, the violence between siblings or the violence done to the teens themselves invariably predicts how they will respond when, for instance, Johnny pushes them off the playground swing," he says.

Only 18% say their parents are "very strict" about what they are permitted to watch on TV.

Violence, Dr. McAfee insists, is a learned behavior. We learn it from infancy up, and its patterns are reinforced over the years. Consequently many of those responsible for the worst crimes, began committing small, stepping-stone crimes by the time they were 10 or 11.

Copying parent behavior "is still the most teachable part of that child's life," says Dr. McAfee. "If you embrace violence by striking out at others, by your language, by condoning violence or laughing at it, then understand that that's what you as a teacher are conveying to your children."

Realize that Violence Does Not Work

Dr. Gelles believes the first step to curbing violence in the home is simply through realizing that it does not work. "Even the milder forms of physical and verbal abuse are harmful in the long run. So if you want your child to have good self-esteem, you really have to abandon physical punishment. You wouldn't want your boss to do it to you. Why do it to your teen?"

In fact, Dr. Gelles' organization defines family violence as any form of injurious behavior toward a family member that would be unacceptable and even illegal toward a stranger. "If you can't inflict such behavior on a stranger, why would you want to inflict it on the most important people in your life?" asks Dr. Gelles.

"I don't think this happens in most of my friends' houses," says Tom, a senior at a suburban high school, "but my parents treat me like an adult, like I am capable of making my decisions. I think that's the way it should be. They have to take control when you're younger, but after a certain level of maturity, that's the way it should be."

The second step toward preventing family violence, says Dr. Gelles, includes developing techniques that allow you as a parent to discipline a child or teen without humiliating them or tearing them down. Far too frequently, Dr. Gelles observes, teens are brought into his office by their parents and identified as the problem in the family, when the problem rests with the parents.

First determine: What makes you angry with your teen? What drives you crazy? What sends your tolerance level over the line such that violence of some form is a possibility? Then figure out how to handle those situations. One of the best ways? "Send yourself to your room. Find something to do to work off your frustration," says Dr. Gelles.

The most effective means to disciplining children and teens are time and reason. Take time to work things out. Reason with your child: "Why are you doing this? What can we do to ease your frustration? Why is it important for you to stop this kind of behavior?" As a parent, keep this in mind: much of the time that the teen is being disciplined, it is because the parent has a problem, not the teen.

But what about the simple fact of teens being difficult to deal with, even impossible? Dr. Gelles has a down-to-earth response. "Well, that's part of the developmental stage. Your kid is going to be obnoxious. Teens have to be obnoxious. He's going to think you are a moron. He's going to think he knows everything." What can you do about this particular teen scourge? Dr. Gelles answers with a chuckle, "Not a lot."

THE EXPERTS SUM IT UP

- Contact teachers and principals in a friendly letter; provide phone numbers where you can be reached at all times.

- Talk with the school about a safety program at your school — about walking children to and from schools, about hallway patrols.

- Know your child's friends and their parents. Ask for phone numbers and addresses.

- Turn media violence into an opportunity for discussion: Ask your children how they would respond to a situation, or, was there a better resolution than the one depicted, for example.

- Violence — hitting, verbal abuse, shunning — is not an effective means of raising children.

- Violence is a learned behavior. If children see it at home, they will practice it later.

- Develop alternative responses to disruptive behavior; reason with your child, discuss the fallout of their behavior, demonstrate the behaviors yourself that you would like them to use.

- Stop to consider why you are really angry — is it the child, or is it you?

- Accept the reality that you and your kids will occasionally drive each other crazy.

- Seek outside counsel when a situation seems unmanageable.

CHAPTER 2

Teen Sex — Will Kids Heed The Warnings?

REALITY: The twin threats of unwanted teen pregnancies and AIDS make teen sexuality more complicated — and more dangerous — than ever.

Perhaps nothing approaches human sexuality's mix of attractions, prohibitions and implications. This is particularly true for teens, who today face not only the same sexual pressures, concerns and mind-games that have plagued people for centuries, but now, add the very real and frightening hazard of sexually transmitted diseases. AIDS hangs ominously over the whole area. Few discussions about teen sexuality these days seem to take place without reference to it, adding a dimension of fear to one of the most basic and natural of human biological functions.

On top of everything, teens wander into this mine field at a time when they are rejecting their parents' guidance more often than not. They are trying on the fit of their almost-adult psyches and in many cases need to rely on their own counsel — and the counsel of peers. Yet the results of any missteps can be so very disastrous. It is no wonder that parents want to have a clear say in their teen's sexual development.

"The atmosphere of the typical high school has become highly sexualized, so that kids feel that sexuality is an enormously invasive and disruptive feature of school life," says Dr. Thomas Lickona, education professor and author of "Sex, Love and You: Making the Right Decision."

"We're living in a culture now where sex is out of control in many ways, and that problem is reflected in young people. And by any reasonable measure," Dr. Lickona adds, "we could say that sex education in this country for the last two decades has been a public health failure."

Sex Education — a Public Health Failure?

How do teens feel about the two most pernicious results of that alleged failure: unwanted teen pregnancy, and AIDS? By and large, they favor more education, more information, more instruction. The vast majority of teens do not feel that teaching abstinence alone — without also teaching an alternative — has any lasting value for them. Yet there are some pressing reasons to discourage teen sexual activity altogether, and these arguments must be heard as well.

The experts we interviewed for this chapter were careful to couch their advice in a way that allows for natural sexual development. While the dangers must be stressed, they said, teens still need to puzzle out their own development, so that as mature adults, partners and spouses, they will have a healthy attitude toward this natural and fulfilling part of life.

That is an important attribute. Because the majority of teens today look forward with great enthusiasm to marriage, loving sexual relationships, and children. Recent Gallup Youth Surveys have found that most teens have the same hopes for marriage and children as did their parents and grandparents.

For example, 88% of teens hope to marry someday, and 84% hope to have children. These figures represent an

> *"We're living in a culture now where sex is out of control in many ways."*

increased optimism toward marriage and parenthood. When we ran a similar survey in 1977, we found that 84% hoped to marry while 79% planned to have children.

There is no gender disparity of note in these findings. Among women, 88% hope to marry while 86% of males hope to marry. Regarding children, 45% of teens would like to have two or more kids in their family, and 9% would like four or more children.

What is important to remember from these findings, say our experts, is that while we are lecturing and bombarding teens with scarifying information on pregnancy and AIDS, we must also remember to permit the development of positive, healthy, natural feelings toward sex.

Unwanted Teen Pregnancy, the Perennial Problem

According to the Alan Guttmacher Institute, which does research on reproductive issues, one in 11 abortions performed in this country is performed on a woman age 18 or under. That encompasses a lot of teen-agers, including many who have mixed feelings toward abortion.

Like the rest of the country, the teen population is divided on this subject. Nearly half of all teens (46%) support abortion rights. But over a third (37%) feel abortion should not be permissible under any circumstances. That does not leave much room for compromise. The percentage of support has not changed appreciably in recent years, although those who object to abortion under any circumstances have dropped from 44% in 1991 to the current 37%.

Regardless of their positions, teens believe they should receive education both on what their abortion rights are and on abstinence. Some 64% of teens feel this way and six teens in 10 (59%) believe that abstinence should be taught for those who are not married. Yes, abstinence, a startling finding to some.

Given the hypothetical prospect of a young, unmarried pregnant woman, teens were asked to rate a variety of her options on a grade of excellent to poor. Few of the options received a strong rating of excellent, probably because teens do not think there is anything "excellent" about teen pregnancy. They feel the most excellent option of all would be no unwanted pregnancies in the first place.

TEENS DIVIDED ON ABORTION

Favor allowing a woman to have an abortion for any reason she chooses	46%
Favor outlawing abortion for any reason	37%

That said, almost all favored a course of action other than abortion. The highest percentage of teens (47%) favored the young woman putting her child up for adoption. Some 43% said she ought to have the child, and another 37% said the acceptability of this situation would improve if the father agreed to marry her right away. Only 16% said having an abortion was a "good" option; 59% felt it was a poor option.

There was a clear difference in the attitudes of white and black teens. Among white teens, adoption was by far the best alternative for unwanted teen pregnancies (52% chose it); only 19% of young black teens

Six teens in ten believe that abstinence should be taught for those who are not married.

agreed, perhaps aware of the greater difficulty in placing minority children in adoptive homes. Young black teens were far more supportive of unwed teen mothers.

In general, teens do not believe that their peers make good, responsible parents. They believe that the age of 20 is about the lowest for young women to succeed at parenting. The age of acceptability for fathers is 22. Only 4% of teens think women ages 16 and younger are responsible enough for parenthood, and only 2% of teens think that of men 16 and younger.

How to prevent this hypothetical scenario of too-early parenthood from enveloping your teen? As in everything else, the experts say, start young, say it often, and reinforce what you believe so your teen has no doubts about your position.

How Do I Say No?

For its national pregnancy prevention program, The Planned Parenthood Federation of America retains a group of national teen consultants who regularly apprise them on what is happening on the front line of teen sexuality. "Start teaching at a young age" is their unrelenting message. While they do not want adults to give up on them just because they are older, adults and parents need to start providing children with messages of conduct from the time they are able to talk.

What messages are young people looking for? Among the experts we talked with is Tijuana James-Traore, who directs the Federation's national pregnancy-prevention program "First Things First." She said that teens want messages on how to negotiate relationships. It is a simple but earnest request. Most teens are entering serious romantic relationships for the first time in their lives. The issue of sex overwhelms them, and they are at a loss as to how to conduct themselves.

"Instead of always focusing solely on anatomy and physiology and how pregnancy happens and abortion, they want to know, 'How do I really say no?' They need models for how people relate to one another within the context of a relationship," says Ms. James-Traore. "They don't have the skills yet at that point in their lives, and parents have not been able to model that kind of behavior for them."

In short, telling kids to "Just Say No" does little or nothing, says Ms. James-Traore. Teen relationships are as charged emotionally and physically as are adult relationships. Saying "No" is often a pat response that parents think will work for their teens even where it may not be sufficient in their own relationships. After all, human interaction is more complicated than this.

Some of the most frequently asked questions about teen sexuality are, "When will I be ready for sex?" and "How do I know it's time to do something?"

"These are really important questions and we hear them all the time," says Ms. James-Traore. "But there is really no straight answer to this. Parents need to help their kids determine that. They need to have discussions on this, to provide their ideas for guidance and model some behaviors that teens can use in their own lives."

"That may not always lead to the decision that parents would like their teens to make," she adds, "but at least they have more information and more negotiating skills than they had before."

"Part of the problem, however," warns Ms. James-Traore, "is that many adults do not have the knowledge about sexuality, and are uncomfortable discussing it. When parents do not know the answer to something, they should turn the question into an opportunity. Go ahead and

> *Teens want to know,*
> *"How do I really say no?"*

say to them, 'I don't know the answer to that question. Why don't we look it up together? Why don't we call someone and find out?'"

As far as parental discomfort goes, says Ms. James-Traore, your child's emotional and physical well-being can be at stake here. In short, be an adult and rise above it.

Fathers Play an Important Role

Society needs to do a much better job with adolescent men, our experts say. Fathers and adult men are partly at fault. All too often they laugh, wink and nudge each other, and make jokes when the issue of sex arises, as if there is nothing serious to be discussed, says Ms. James-Traore. This is a real mistake because it trivializes sexuality and at the same time cuts off an opportunity for discussion.

So says 17-year-old Frank, a senior at a high school just outside of Philadelphia, Pa. "Are you kidding? My father never talks about this stuff with me. He told me to buy *Penthouse* if I wanted to know anything about sex. Everything I do know

now, I got from friends. And yeah, some from school too. But who listens to that crap in class?"

Another problem in dealing with younger men, says Ms. James-Traore, is that the emphasis is so often on the image of Male Teen As Perpetrator. This also must stop. "We tend to see young men basically as the perpetrators of pregnancy, and they tend to feel that this is all their sexuality is about," says Ms. James-Traore. "What they want to know is, what really is my role in all of this? And I think we have to help them clarify and understand that. We tend to focus too much on the adolescent females, and that's why we haven't seen a significant downward trend in the teen pregnancy rate."

Alternate Message: You Are not Ready

Author Dr. Thomas Lickona takes a different approach. He feels teens need to get the message that they are simply not yet ready for sex. Any equivocation of that message, he says, is a green light for teens to go ahead with their impulses and the consequences be damned.

"We'd like to teach young people that learning about another person's values, beliefs, goals and qualities as a human being are ways to get to know a person apart from sexual knowledge," says Dr. Lickona. "This kind of conduct in a teen relationship can satisfy the yearning for intimacy without involving a young couple in a physical relationship."

One of the ways Dr. Lickona would like to see that happen is through classroom discussions about relationships on a level that teens can understand. Teens are sick of hearing stories about teen pregnancy and AIDS, he says. However, tell them a story about a relationship that went horribly wrong and the emotional fallout that was suffered, and their attention is riveted.

"It's harder for a 15- and 16-year-old to relate to a story about pregnancy or disease. They may never have had a big-time disease. They may never have been pregnant or know anyone their age who was," says Dr. Lickona. "But everybody's feelings have been hurt, everybody's been mistreated or rejected. So kids can relate immediately to the feelings

TAUGHT IN SCHOOL	
How to prevent getting AIDS	93%
How AIDS is caught	91%
Discussions about safe sex	86%
Abstinence	76%

of people who have regrets about having sex with their first boyfriend, or having exploited and hurt others."

The value of such stories, says Dr. Lickona, is that they demonstrate how much there is at stake in any relationship. It gives teens pause, something to reflect on, and a sense of the gravity of the situation. Consequently, their behavior will be less impulsive, and arise from a more mature level of thought.

AIDS: What Should We Teach?

By the time your teen has turned age 17, he or she has invariably had at least general classroom instruction on how one can contract AIDS and how to prevent it. Our surveys, in fact, show that 97% of America's teens have been thus educated. Another 93% have had some level of specific, classroom AIDS instruction. Safe sex, or the use of condoms, has been discussed in school with 91% of teens ages 16 and older, and 83% of teens between the ages of 13 and 15.

And regardless of how their parents may feel about it, 82% of teens think condoms should be distributed at their high schools.

Right now, 9% of teens tell us that condoms are available in their schools. Are they using them? Or is it just someone else's problem?

A recent survey by the United States Centers for Disease Control and Prevention among 16,000 high school students found that 53% had engaged in sexual intercourse at least once — a percentage that has remained virtually unchanged in the 1990s. But condom use has increased among them, the CDC said. In 1993, 53% of students said they had used a condom the last time they had sex, compared with 46% when a similar survey was conducted in 1991.

By a ratio of two to one, according to our Gallup Youth Surveys, teens believe that sex education should focus more on safe sex than on abstinence as a means of avoiding AIDS (although, as noted earlier, 59% of teens think abstinence should be taught for teens as part of sex education).

> *"53% of high school students have engaged in sexual intercourse."*
> **U.S. Centers for Disease Control** survey of 16,000 teens.

Since teens are fairly clear about the link between how they are behaving and what they need to know, why are adults so torn up about what to teach their adolescents?

Dr. Lickona believes educational efforts are misleading teens — and the society in general — with the safety assurances of condoms. "Sex education today is where kids are told, you've got two choices: Abstinence is the only foolproof method but you can be safer by the consistent use of condoms. And for teens, that represents a green light. It sends a mixed message: Don't have sex but here's a safe way to do it if you do. That's extremely deceptive and there are enormous risks physically, emotionally and spiritually for kids who engage," he says.

Dr. Lickona favors teaching teens that the only way to conduct sex safely is within a monogamous, committed, adult relationship — preferably one in which the two partners are married. To each other. On the other side of the fence are those who believe that teens are going to engage in sex regardless of what they are taught, and that information and education is as necessary as arming one's self before battle.

Both sides have a point, and both sides need to be heard.

One advocate of education is Trish Moylan-Torruella, Vice President for Education at The Planned Parenthood Federation of America. "We feel very strongly that if we come at kids either denying that they are sexual or with a 'Just Say No' message, then we end up losing credibility with them. They reply, 'You have nothing to say to me because you're not willing to admit that there is something wonderful about sexual activity.'"

Lisa is a senior at a middle-class suburban high school. She has been dating her boyfriend for nearly two years, and says their sexual relationship started a few months after they met. "Of course we have had sex. I knew we would almost as soon as I started dating him. It wasn't a question of pressure or anything. It just seemed like the natural thing to do. It is for parents. Why shouldn't it be for us, too?"

The Federation endorses teaching about sexuality — and its risks — within a positive context, primarily because it believes that is a message to which teens will both listen and respond. "If you're constantly focusing on, have sex, get AIDS, die, it's hardly going to send out a positive message that teens will listen to," says Ms. Torruella. "With good information, you can prevent the risks. We're not promoting sexual activity. But we believe that abstinence is one choice among many. The important thing is to equip young people to make the right decisions about what is right for them."

Lessons Learned Over a Lifetime

"Adults need to realize that sexuality does not begin at puberty," says Ms. Torruella. "It begins at birth, as soon as we start imparting messages about what it means to be female or male. Parents should take note of how they are transmitting those messages, and what those messages are. When a young child asks a question about sexuality and parents become nervous or deflect the question," she told us, "that sends a powerful statement about the mystery and unapproachability of sex.

"Be thoughtful and comfortable in dealing with your growing child's sexuality," advised Ms. Torruella, "and they will in turn be comfortable with themselves. Partner consistency is also important," she says. "Children and teens should not get mixed messages from their parents about what kinds of behavior are endorsed. Sexuality is confusing enough. Straighten the issues out with your partner before they arise with your children."

Ms. Torruella also believes that parents should remember that information does not necessarily lead to behavior. "Suppose I say to my child, 'When your reproductive system is ready, you could get pregnant. The way people prevent that is through methods of birth control. Here are some. But I don't think it's a good idea for you to have sex before marriage.' Why is that such an intolerable message?"

"Giving information is not transmitting values. Some parents think that by withholding information, they're going to keep their kids safe. Kids have a very healthy need to learn about sex. And if you don't tell them, they're sure going to go somewhere else," says Ms. Torruella.

There is a phrase used often in Planned Parenthood programs. It is "teachable moments," and it refers to those moments in life when opportunities arise naturally to discuss or highlight a particular topic. Regarding both unwanted pregnancies and the threat of AIDS, Planned Parenthood experts advise parents to watch for and seize these moments, turning them into an exchange of information between parent and child.

Such moments could involve those ubiquitous playground comments your children come home with —"Timmy said this on the playground today. What did he mean?" They could spring from subjects children are working on in school. They could arise out of commercials on television, music your child is listening to, predicaments of friends.

> *"Some parents think that by withholding information, they're going to keep their kids safe. But giving information is not transmitting values."*

Parents must be alert for these opportunities, and then broach topics with simple questions like, "What do you think?" or "How would you respond to that?" Teachable moments strengthen not only the parent-child bond, but give both sides a chance to clarify their positions. Honestly. Forthrightly.

"It's a tough time to be an adolescent and a tough time to be a parent," says Ms. Torruella. "That means it's very important to focus on the positive, on what we can do. And it's important to know that there is help out there for you. There is something wrong with knowing you have a problem and not doing anything about it."

And there is something both teens and parents can do —
the experts agree. Communicate!

THE EXPERTS SUM IT UP

* Remind young people often that the best way to
  conduct sex safely is within a monogamous,
  committed adult relationship.

* Sexuality begins at birth, not at puberty. Monitor the
  messages you give young children and teens on what
  it means to be female, what it means to be male.

* Provide models on how teens can conduct
  themselves responsibly in a relationship.

* Help your teens answer such questions as, "How do
  I say 'No'?" and "When will I be ready for sex?" by
  discussing your own philosophy.

* Take advantage of those occasional "Teachable
  Moments."

* Do not be afraid to admit you do not know the
  answer to something. Offer to look for the answer
  with your teen.

* Treat sexuality as a normal, healthy but serious
  subject. Jokes about sexuality are inappropriate.

* Young males need models on their roles as well as
  on how sex affects them in ways other than
  unwanted pregnancies.

* Abstinence remains the only foolproof guarantee for
  safe sex. Teens need to understand this and to know
  that it is an option that many follow.

* Yet information fitting the range of decisions they
  can make is just as necessary, and information does
  not necessarily lead to behavior.

CHAPTER 3

Health, Sleep, Exercise and Diet — Future Heart Victims?

REALITY: Bad eating habits, not enough sleep, poor attitudes toward exercise and too much fatty food combine to put America's teens on a dangerous path.

B ad eating habits are a universal teen trait, almost a badge of honor. You are a teen, ergo you eat poorly — partly for spite, partly because your body is younger and more tolerant of nutritional abuse than it will be in a decade or more. Considering all the problems teens are facing today, who can begrudge them the simple pleasures of junk food and weekends, on the couch, watching MTV?

Many authorities do just that, as it turns out, and with good reason, too. More today than perhaps ever, we are coming to understand the importance of early nutrition and exercise and their implications for an individual's health over a lifetime. The health of the body as a mature adult, as a middle-aged person and even as a senior citizen often has its genesis in the habits of adolescent and teen years, according to the health experts we spoke with, such as former Surgeon General C. Everett Koop, and American Medical Association President Robert McAfee.

As society in general pricks up its ears at this message, so in turn do its teen-agers. Our survey findings indicate that nearly two out of three are aware these days about the value of good nutrition and exercise. This is far greater than the proportion of their peers just 15 years ago.

They Know More; Do They Practice It?

Given a lengthy list of items in a recent Gallup Youth Survey about what might be important for teens to know, a solid majority ranked nutritional awareness fairly high on the list. Along with "achieving college" and "knowing how to invest and handle one's money," some 60% of teens said nutritional knowledge is very important. Another 37% said it is somewhat important.

SELF-IMAGE		
	Girls	**Boys**
Currently dieting	24%	5%
Would like to lose weight	53%	19%
Satisfied with appearance	37%	46%

Ultimately, then, nearly every teen-ager (97%) is at least aware of the importance of good nutrition.

When it comes to eating well, young women are far more at-risk than young men. One teen-age girl in four (24%) is dieting compared with 5% of young men, according to recent survey findings. More than half of young women (53%) would like to lose weight, an inclination that is often the result of unrealistic standards about how they ought to look. Only 19% of males say this. At the same time, about half of all young men

(46%) are pleased with their weight and appearance, but only 37% of young women.

And while most teens continue to eat dinner with their families — where they are most likely to meet nutritional requirements because their parents have control over what is in front of them — far more young men (82%) eat this meal with their families than do young women (68%). Breakfast is a lower priority for both young men and young women — only two teens in three (65%) say they usually eat breakfast.

Here is a snatch of a "he said/she said" conversation from a recent teen focus group Gallup held at an upscale suburban high school on health, exercise and nutrition. It stands as a fairly reliable synopsis of how teen-agers — both male and female — approach the issues of nutrition and exercise in their lives:

JOHN: "I pay attention to nutrition, but I do accept the fact that just because of my physical makeup, I can pretty much eat whatever I want, and I'll never show it. I guess that's not a bad problem to have. And I understand nutrition, but I don't do anything about it right now."

SARAH: "I'm the complete opposite. I had to accept that no matter what I do, I'm not going to be a five-foot, eleven-inch model with long skinny legs. So I pay attention to nutrition, I worry about it, I do my best. It's hard being in school. If you walk down to the cafeteria and see what they offer, I mean, you might as well just go outside and eat grass. I think 17-year-olds usually know something about nutrition, but it's hard to do something about it at this point."

TRACEY: "Last year in AP Biology, we had to do an analysis of our diet for a week. And it was really amazing at the end. You were like, did I really eat that? I did a 110% turn-around after that. When you see it, you realize you don't get enough carbohydrates or vegetables, and too much protein. I really slowed down and took a look at my eating habits after that."

ROBERT: "Actually I ate even more after that..."

Obesity among adolescents and teen-agers is on the rise. So much so, in fact, that the Centers for Disease Control have established as a primary goal for the year 2000 limiting obesity among 12- to 19-year-olds to only 15% of this age group.

Fatigue — a Trigger for Trouble?

Teens, along with many of today's pressured adults, push themselves beyond their limits, and a majority of teens say that fatigue is a concern among their peers. Some 52% report that they often do not have the energy to concentrate on homework at the end of the day because they are simply too tired.

This could be a function of exhaustion — six out of 10 teens awaken between 6 and 7 a.m. each morning for school and then have the same long day of activi-

52% of teens say they can't concentrate on homework because they are too tired.

ties that most adults experience. But teens also agree that fatigue can be the result of poor conditioning, poor diets and little or no exercise.

Whichever is cause and whichever effect, there is growing

awareness that young people, strained by fatigue, are more likely to engage in risky behavior, whether this is skipping classes to catch up on sleep or to avoid tests for which they are not prepared, or more physically harmful behavior such as alcohol abuse or drug experimentation.

Persistent fatigue may be a trigger for more trouble than teens or their parents realize, and perhaps one of the risks easiest to avoid.

Can't Run a Mile

Now look at the exercise habits of teens. Because of gym classes and the abundance of sports programs at most schools, teens are more likely to be exposed to a variety of exercise opportunities than are their parents. This, however, does not mean that they are taking advantage of those opportunities.

On the surface, the findings appear to be promising.

While 74% of male teens play on team sports, only 47% of female teens do.

Most teens (98% of boys and 94% of girls) exercise at least once a week, and the majority play on sports teams, take gym class, or participate in some other form of exercise. Still, a class or two each week does not make a fit and healthy young body. If there is no regular commitment to exercise, then there is no fitness.

There are two disturbing health trends emerging among teens. One, a recent survey by the American Medical Association, "America's Adolescents: How Healthy Are They?" found that the majority of children and adolescents are in poor physical shape. Specifically, for instance, more than half of all girls and a quarter of all boys are unable to do a single pull-up.

Again, half of all young women and 30% of all young men are unable to run a mile in less than 10 minutes.

"Poor performance on cardiorespiratory (heart-lung) endurance tests is related to early fatigue in intellectual and physical activities and can contribute to the development of heart disease in life," according to the report.

The other trend is already evidenced by the findings above: Young women are far less likely to exercise regularly than are young men. Perhaps that is a matter of choice, but fewer opportunities and less encouragement to take part in organized sports programs may also explain this gender gap.

The mass media is as much to blame here as teens themselves — particularly the kinds of media indulged in by young women. Magazines for young men encourage them to shoot rapid rivers, learn hiking and climbing skills, play football, ride mountain bikes. Yet the idea of adventurous or exciting activities for young women put forward in their magazines all too often involves getting a new haircut or buying a little slip of a dress. Hardly a prescription for fitness and outdoor activity.

This attitude is reflected in young women's sports activities, particularly at school. While 74% of male teens play on team sports, only 47% of female teens do; 72% of young men go to gym class regularly, 63% of young women do; 60% of young men train with weights, but only 29% of young females; 40% of young males play individual sports such as tennis, but only 26% of females.

Weighing in as an advocate of teen exercise — for both genders, on a regular and sustained basis — is Tom McMillen, Co-Chair (with Florence Griffith Joyner) of the President's Council on Physical Fitness in Washington, D.C. Mr. McMillen talked with us about some of his frustrations and hopes.

"In the information age, the ascendance of Nintendo and computers and all that has kept kids more sedentary. And of course television — the average child spends the equivalent of one to two years of school life watching television. That's a pretty debilitating force when you're trying to promote the President's physical fitness objectives," says Mr. McMillen.

Thirty Minutes Every Day

The Council's objectives for American fitness are straightforward. While the Council does not break down fitness objectives based on age groups, Mr. McMillen says he would like to see every teen in the country exercising for at least 30 minutes each day. There is a misconception among both parents and their teens that teenagers do not need to take additional steps to get in

> *"The average child spends the equivalent of one to two years of school life watching television."*

shape, that they are simply blessed, by virtue of age and energy level, with more cardiovascular fitness.

This could not be farther from the truth. For one thing, Mr. McMillen explains, good exercise habits adopted in the teen years have more of a tendency to last over an individual's life than those adopted later, by adults. For another, teens who are involved in sports and in physical health are less likely to fall prey to drug abuse, cigarette smoking and even, he says, to the lure of violent behavior. The Council has done numerous studies linking the decline in physical fitness to juvenile delinquency and cigarette and drug abuse habits.

"There are many different ways to exercise, and it is easy to get in 30 minutes a day. That's not a lot of time, particularly for a teen-ager," says Mr. McMillen. "We encourage people to walk up steps, or walk to work or school if possible. Do you have a dog? Your dog needs exercise. Walk or run your dog before school and after."

Parents can take a pro-active role in seeing that their teens get enough exercise — with some hearty benefits accruing to them, as well. Exercising together is one way of spending more time with the members of your family, says Mr. McMillen. Go out and run together. Walk through the park together. Turn off the television and invite your teen to recreate with you.

SELF-IMAGE		
Form of exercise	Females	Males
Team sports	47%	74%
Gym class	63%	72%
Jogs or runs once a week	50%	61%
Works out with weights	29%	60%
Bicycles once a week	31%	41%
Individual sports, like tennis	26%	40%
No activity last week	6%	2%

"One of the problems with families today is that they go out and spectate instead of recreate," says Mr. McMillen. "So instead of going to the football game with your kids, take them on a hike. Go out and go skiing for the day or the weekend instead of watching 'Wide World of Sports' on television. These kinds of activities set a pattern for your child's life all the way through."

He also urges teens and parents to reject the prevailing attitude that one's body goes into serious decline as one ages. This is simply not written in stone, Mr. McMillen says. Individuals have a great deal more control over their physical health than perhaps they like to admit. "There is no excuse for a sedentary lifestyle, especially when you're a teen. But really," he says, "at any age."

"How to get started?" he asks, posing his own leading question. Answer: The President's Council on Physical Fitness has innumerable pamphlets and resources explaining how to bring more exercise into your home. Or, more simply, walk out the front door with your teen, just keep going and come back together.

Comprehensive Health for Teens

"The major problem with Americans from a public health point of view is that we tell people to do things when it's already too late," says Dr. Koop. "We tell people to watch what they eat and to exercise after they are already obese. We tell them they shouldn't smoke after

"I would like to see every teen in the country exercising for at least 30 minutes each day."

they have lung disease. We tell them not to drink after they already have a drinking problem. We tell them to exercise after they have problems with their heart."

The American Medical Association, with Dr. Robert McAfee at its helm, apparently could not agree more. Consequently the Association has developed a comprehensive list of preventive procedures and recommendations aimed at adolescents, which its members hope will cut down on disease and illness as the current group of teens age. They call the program GAPS — Guidelines for Adolescent Preventive Services. In long form, it is available to all AMA-member doctors, hospitals and health-care providers. Abbreviated versions of the program are available to the public for the asking.

The overall thrust of GAPS is to involve the family's doctor or health-care giver in preventive counseling that educates both the parent and the teen-ager, and does it partly on the basis of teen confidentiality. This element might upset some parents, who want to retain control over the health-care advice their teens are receiving. Dr. McAfee explains the reason for it.

"GAPS is certainly not meant to interfere in the parent-child relationship," he says. "At the same time, we're finding that adolescents are much more resembling adults than they are resembling children in their behavior, in their risk-taking, in their decisions to behave in such a way that their lives may be threatened. And in this regard, if we're talking about preventive information, then the exchange of information for some adolescents may be the most effective way to prevent premature death.

"So the confidentiality issue is essentially out of respect for the patient, who happens to be approaching the age of majority," Dr. McAfee adds. "It's really an attempt to help parents parent."

In short, GAPS promotes 24 recommendations for adolescent health-care, administered primarily by the family doctor. The program should form the basis of a partnership between adolescent, family doctor and parent. Most of the recommendations include health screenings that back up the recommendations, and provide laboratory confirmation to parent and teen that all is going well.

24 Steps to Health and Fitness

The 24-step program provides information on a gamut of issues that affect teens: puberty and adolescence, sexuality, the risks of smoking and drinking, emotional health, drug abuse, learning disabilities and family violence. Here are some of the recommendations related to exercise and nutrition:

- "From ages 11 to 21, all adolescents should have an annual preventive visit with a doctor."
- "Physicians should establish office policies regarding confidential care for adolescents and how parents will be involved in that care."
- "Parents or other adult caregivers should receive health guidance at least once during their child's early adolescence, once during middle adolescence and, preferably, once during late adolescence."
- "All adolescents should receive health guidance annually about dietary habits, including the benefits of a healthy diet, and ways to achieve a healthy diet and safe weight management."
- "All adolescents should receive health guidance annually about the benefits of exercise and should be encouraged to engage in safe exercise on a regular basis."
- "Selected adolescents should be screened to determine their risk of developing hyperlipidemia and adult coronary heart disease." (For example, teens whose parents have high serum cholesterol levels, adolescents whose parents or grandparents have coronary artery diseases, and any adolescents with unknown family histories.)
- "All adolescents should be screened annually for eating disorders and obesity by determining weight and stature, and asking about body image and dieting patterns."

In sum, GAPS provides for a blanket of recommendations that help ensure the health of today's teen-agers. And because it springs from a family physician's office — one of the most trusted sources of involvement in family matters — the AMA feels the program has a greater chance of success. So that as teens age, early health intervention will pay off in healthier adults and elderly citizens.

"By and large, if you think about how medical care has been delivered in this country, there's never been any great focus on the adolescent," says Dr. McAfee. "We have strong commitments to neonatal care and pediatrics. Then internal medicine and family practices begin focusing on the older population.

"This is what motivated the AMA to look at what we're not doing, and what we can create that can form a fabric for any physician who wants to have a more significant impact on young Americans. It's an attempt to create a relationship for adolescents with a primary caregiver, with the family and the parents as critical players."

THE EXPERTS SUM IT UP

- Don't let fatigue push your teen into trouble. Exhaustion can be a dangerous trigger!

- Encourage young women to participate in extracurricular sports programs to the same degree as young men.

- Require teens to eat breakfast and dinner with the family, where adults can supervise their nutritional intake.

- Idea: Set a family pattern of commitment to physical exercise.

- Idea: Set a goal of 30 minutes of exercise each day for the family's teens.

- Recreate, rather than spectate; go hiking together instead of watching a football game together.

- Walk or run with the family dog each day.

- Involve your family doctor in preventive health-care either through the GAPS program or yearly counseling sessions and screenings.

- Teens should have some access to confidential health-care counseling, with the blessings of the parent.

CHAPTER 4

Drugs, Cigarettes, Alcohol, Suicide — Still Huge Problems

REALITY: Drug and alcohol abuse, rampant among teens in this country, are linked not only to higher rates of juvenile crime but also to rising rates of teen suicide.

We lecture teens in this society long and hard about drug abuse, about the dangers of marijuana, cocaine and other dangerous drugs. Yet our billboards, our magazine ads and our television commercials are splashed with hip young drinkers and smokers having the time of their (abbreviated) lives. Does this make sense?

Recent Gallup Youth Survey findings indicate that teens are getting both of these distinct messages. On the one hand, only a fraction of teens think hard drugs are a real concern in their lives, so the majority are heeding the message and avoiding these drugs. But alcohol and cigarettes are another matter altogether, proving that teens are being seduced by the ads. It is time to shatter a few popularly held notions about the controlled substances that truly threaten the majority of American teen-agers.

Far and away, alcohol and cigarettes enter and influence teens' lives more frequently than do hard drugs. We will take a closer look at the hard facts below, but it's important to note right up front that close to half of today's teen-agers say that drinking and smoking are problems among peers, with 46% of teens saying alcohol consumption is a problem and 43% saying cigarette smoking is a problem.

The percentage of teens who worry about marijuana use? A far lower 29%. The percentage who worry about the use of hard drugs? Only 16%. This would seem to suggest that our society is either placing a much harsher (though certainly correct) taboo on the less-pervasive controlled substances, or dangerously understating the problems of those that are readily available to nearly every teen.

There is another misconception to be shattered here, one involving the presence of suicide in the lives of teens and the often conflicting speculations about what causes it. As it turns out, according to teen reports, suicide is prompted not by heavy metal music, not by satanic rituals, not even by the computer games such as "Dungeons and Dragons." The two biggest factors, teens tell us, are substance abuse and problems at home.

In this chapter, we focus on the risks that teens choose — drugs, alcohol, cigarettes and suicide — which are linked in the minds and actions of American teen-agers. First we review our survey findings and prescriptions from experts for alcohol, drug and cigarette abuse, then we turn to the tragic problem of suicide.

Drugs, Alcohol, Cigarettes: Everyday Dangers

According to our teen surveys, alcohol usage has declined among American teen-agers in a time period that happens to coincide with the time since the drinking age was raised to a uniform 21 years of age. Today, 21% of teens say they drink regularly, compared to 41% of teens who reported the same habits in 1982. Alcohol usage has dropped to about the level it was among teens in the 1950s.

Close to half of American teens feel drinking is a problem among their peers.

Still, these numbers may be a bit optimistic. Nearly half (46%) of American teen-agers feel drinking is a problem among their peers, and this proportion rises to 57% among teens ages 16 and 17. Only 3% of these teens have permission from their parents to drink or are permitted to drink around them, so clearly the behavior is persisting against parental wishes.

And, although tougher drinking and driving laws have contributed to reducing the number of alcohol-related driving deaths, 21% of teens say they have been in a car at least once with someone their age who was under the influence of alcohol.

Also discouraging is the fact that teens still have relatively easy access to alcohol. About half — 48% of teens — say it is very easy to buy, and 31% say it is fairly easy to buy. That means nearly 80% of teens have few problems getting their hands on alcohol. And not just the older teens. Nearly 40% of teens between the ages of 13 and 15 say they likewise have no trouble getting alcohol.

What are they buying? Beer, beer and beer. Three out of four teens who drink, drink beer. It is also the most commonly available alcohol in American households.

Speaking of those households, one teen in five reports that drinking is a problem in their family now, and some 7% of teens fear that alcohol may be a problem for them one day as well.

A New Generation of Tobacco Addicts

A new generation of tobacco addicts is coming of age, significantly at a time when adults are quitting at unsurpassed rates.

Some 43% of teens are concerned about cigarette smoking, while a national average of about 14% of all teens smoke regularly. Seven teens in 10 who smoke say they would not start again if they had the chance; two in three want to quit but have not; half have tried to quit but cannot; four in 10 light up within one hour of waking in the morning; 66% of teens who smoke would like to stop. Now.

What do teens feel would help them cut down on their habits? For one thing, cost. Asked recently if a $1 or $2 surtax on a pack of cigarettes would have any effect on their habit, three out of four teen smokers say they would be forced to cut back significantly, if not stop smoking altogether. Some 63% of teens who don't smoke also say cost is a primary factor. They simply cannot afford the habit.

Limiting one's ability to smoke, teens say, also may have some effect. Three teens out of four feel smoking should be prohibited on school grounds (for both students and teachers), and most support the prohibitions in public restaurants and shopping malls.

> *Three out of four teens who smoke say a heavy tax on cigarettes would force them to cut back significantly or quit altogether.*

What Turns Teens Off

One group of students who participated in a recent focus group at an affluent suburban high school avidly supported "grotesque" advertisements and health class photographs that show the physical toll of cigarette smoking. "In our health class they showed us distorted body parts from people who smoke and people who chew tobacco," says 17-year-old Yan. "And it just turned me off."

Adds Sarah: "Also, hearing from people who smoke and who can't run half a mile without choking to death. That kinda makes it really real for me."

The same theme was voiced by teens in an inner-city focus group. Asked what kinds of tactics a T.V. commercial might use to persuade them to give up smoking, one teen replied, "Show the gunky lung of someone who has been smoking."

TEENS WHO SMOKE	
Smoke regularly	14%
Among those who smoke:	
Would not start smoking again if given the chance	70%
Want to quit	66%
Have tried to quit	51%

Beyond cigarettes and alcohol lie drugs. Teens feel quite certain about the danger of hard drugs, even if those drugs have less of a presence in the average teen's life today than they might have had 20 years ago. Virtually all teens view crack (99%) and cocaine (98%) as very dangerous, and a large proportion (83%) view marijuana as very dangerous. Just 11% of teens say they have ever smoked marijuana, and the numbers are even lower for the use of substances like crack and LSD. The percentage of regular users of hard drugs is quite low indeed.

Experts concerned about teen health agree that early intervention is key. So, for example, says former United States Surgeon General C. Everett Koop, who in the 1980s was one of the most outspoken opponents of smoking on the national scene. In his talk with us about the advice we could give parents, Dr. Koop remains unequivocal in his denunciation of smoking. But he claims little will work unless parents begin drilling anti-smoking messages into their children long before they become teen-agers.

"People put a tremendous effort into telling 13-year-olds not to smoke. Well, it's too late for most of them, who have already decided. If you try to tell teens not to smoke at the age of 13 or 15, you're whistling Dixie," says Dr. Koop, who today directs the *"Teens are immortal in their own eyes. Nothing can happen to them."* National Safe Kids Campaign headquartered in Washington, D.C. "The same is true of drinking. The same is true of sex. You're dealing with a very special group of people here, and unless you understand them you're going to be frustrated.

"These people are immortal in their own eyes. Nothing can happen to them. Smoking won't bother them; neither will drinking and driving. They don't like health messages. They like to take risks and they don't like anything that begins with the word 'don't!' And unless you get all that straight, you'll never get anywhere."

"Brush Your Teeth, Don't Take Drugs"

How to begin? Start young, the experts say, much younger than the teen years. Start, in fact, when your children are two or three or at least under five. "From the time they can stand up and brush their teeth," says Dr. Koop. If the parents do not smoke and they are clear about why they do not smoke (for example, for health reasons), those messages should be translated as early and as declaratively as possible.

Dr. Koop is less than optimistic about parents who do smoke. Lecturing their children against smoking will do almost nothing, he says, if by their example they are saying something else. Finally, Dr. Koop recommends walking around with children, pointing out people smoking and identifying them as what he believes they are, "drug addicts." That repetition, he insists, will dampen smoking's appeal by the time the youngsters are teens. It worked, he says, with his own grandchildren.

One easy way of inculcating health messages, Dr. Koop says, is by insisting that children develop simple daily habits dedicated to their health. It's the best place to start. "For instance, having your child brush his teeth is a very nice symbol, because it's something he is told to do every day, and it's adult behavior that he can feel good about.

"So you say, here are some things you don't have a choice about. You brush your teeth, you buckle your seatbelts, you eat the diet your parents put in front of you, and you exercise every day. And you will not drink and you will not smoke and you will not take drugs. And that," concludes Dr. Koop, "is a message that you can easily get across to a pre-schooler."

Booze Bigger Problem than Cocaine

Dr. Koop's position regarding alcohol bears out the Gallup Youth Survey findings that alcohol is a much more important problem in high school than cocaine. Like Dr. Koop, Cheryl Perry, the recipient of a grant from the National Institute on

Alcohol Abuse and Addiction, believes the best way to tackle teen alcohol is by starting anti-drinking messages while kids are still kids.

Dr. Perry's "Project Northland" aims to defeat adolescent drinking in school districts throughout Minnesota, where underage drinking is a considerable problem. Project Northland targeted schools, the homes and community bars and liquor stores. The education starts with an anti-alcohol program in sixth-grade classrooms called Slick Tracy and includes work guides and comic books that feature characters trying to combat the social pressures of drinking. One of the project's key lessons, Dr. Perry says, is that in order to be successful, a program must have as comprehensive an application as possible.

> *"We found that about 40% of the fifth-graders had already had alcohol and some were binge drinking by that point."*

"We feel alcohol use and abuse is embedded in the larger social network," says Dr. Perry, a Professor of Epidemiology at the University of Minnesota. "If you just work with the schools, then the kids leave the schools and hang out with their peers and maybe it's easy to get alcohol in the community, and then all your work is undone. It's just not enough to work just with the schools."

But the program, in place for five years, goes beyond books. Teen leaders are trained to reinforce the program from the inside. Seventh-graders produce a play based on an Elvis-type character trying to induce teens to drink. Eighth-graders interview local police, the mayor and other powerful figures in their communities on proposals to reduce alcohol-related influences.

Proactive Parents

Through the parents, home environments are involved. Support materials for each of the programs are taken home and discussed with parents, who are asked to sign booklets as proof of their participation. Parents are also given a list, on which they can note their childrens' friends' names and phone numbers. This harkens back to National Parent-Teacher Association President Kathryn Whitfill's exhortation to know your children's friends.

Finally, the project includes local liquor sellers and bar owners. Merchants were surveyed on sales practices, policies concerning age identification, employee training, the frequency of purchase attempts by minors and perceptions about the availability of liquor to minors in the community. The result, Dr. Perry says, has been a heightened awareness among those on the front line of selling alcohol to the public.

By this point, says Dr. Perry, Project Northland has uncovered several indisputable facts about adolescent drinking. Here is one such major point: "Quite surprisingly, we now think we should have started with fifth-graders," she says. "We found about one third of the kids, about 40%, had already had alcohol and some were binge drinking by that point. We did have a response from parents. They'd say, 'Don't you think it's a little early?' By the end of the sixth-grade programs, parents were saying, 'We had no idea they already knew all this stuff about drinking, and if we'd only known....' "

Suicide and Your Teens

Parents who have experienced a child's suicide never fully recover from the anguish. They remain haunted for the rest of their lives by questions about why a child took his or her life, and if there was truly something that could have been done to prevent it.

In the United States, suicide has become a real teen killer. According to the Centers for Disease Control, the suicide death rate among 15- to 19-year-olds has gone from 2.7 cases per 100,000 in 1950 to 11.1 cases per 100,000 in 1990.

Why? In conjunction with Empire Blue Cross and Blue Shield, and The Gallup Organization, Inc., The Gallup International Institute has conducted two landmark studies this decade to find out. The findings from both are closely matched, suggesting that the profile of suicide among teen-agers remains constant.

> *"The suicide death rate among 15- to 19-year-olds has gone from 2.7 cases per 100,000 in 1950 to 11.1 cases per 100,000 in 1990."*
>
> **U.S. Centers for Disease Control survey of 16,000 teens.**

Teens list the following as the biggest factors in suicide: most point to drug abuse (86%), and to not getting along with parents (84%), along with the pressure of peer activities and stresses (82%). The list continues with problems of growing up (81%), alcohol abuse (71%), satanic cults (65%), problems with school (64%), teen pregnancy (62%), AIDS (56%), teen gangs (53%), and copycat teen suicides (42%).

Judging from our survey findings, teens are no strangers to the existence of suicide in our society. Some 59% of teens say they know someone who has tried to take his or her own life, and 26% know someone who has been successful. More than half of all teens, or 55%, say they have actually discussed the topic of suicide with their friends. And 37% say they have considered taking their lives; 12% of all teens have considered it quite seriously.

When confronted with the potential of suicide — either their own, or suicidal feelings among friends — most teens say they feel comfortable turning to an adult in their lives, with parents or school counselors the most likely choices. If a friend is in trouble, 68% of teens said they would seek advice from their own parents while 53% would tell the parents of the disturbed friend. Another 61% would seek the help of a school counselor; 55% would turn to a suicide hotline; 38% would turn to the clergy; 26% to a teacher. Many teens (40%) also said they would turn to other friends. While these percentages indicate that many teens feel comfortable turning to an adult for help, they also indicate significant percentages who are not comfortable doing so.

We talked with Lanny Berman, Director of the National Center for the Study and Prevention of Suicide at the Washington (D.C.) School of Psychiatry. Adult and teen suicide tends to result most often from some form of depression, says Dr. Berman. The essential difference lies in what triggers that depression.

In both adults and teens, suicide is the end result of overwhelming feelings of rejection, abandonment, fear and/or a sense of loss. But what precipitates those feelings is different for different ages. So, while an adult may become suicidal during a divorce or the loss of a job, teens may become suicidal over a conflict in the family or the breakup with a boyfriend or girlfriend.

The point of this, says Dr. Berman, is that parents need to accept, identify and take seriously teen despondence, because it can have the same devastating effect that adult despondence can — a potential for suicide.

Experts: Take Teen Despondency Seriously

"As adults we tend to have this rather misguided impression that childhood and adolescence should be a time of wonder and awe and discovery and testing the waters. And yes, that's true too, but teen-agers are scared and reactive and sometimes very crazy creatures," says Dr. Berman.

"Our job as adults seems to be to reassure and support," he continues, "but sometimes we act as cheer-leaders when what they really need is a good ear... 'I hear how you feel, let me give you a way of thinking about what's going on so that maybe together, we can help you face this struggle.' "

Parents must be alert, first and foremost, to any mention of suicide, whether verbal or in drawings and writings, says Dr. Berman. The second sign that ought to flag parents' attention is any behavioral communication in which a

TEENS' VIEW OF LEADING CAUSES OF SUICIDE	
Drug abuse	10%
Not getting along with parents	26%
Peer pressure too strong	49%
Problems in growing up	66%
Alcohol abuse	51%
Satanic cults	65%
Problems at school	64%
Teen pregnancy	62%
AIDS	56%
Teen gangs	53%
Copycat teen suicides	42%

child lets a parent know that he or she is "not doing well." They are noticeably sad over a longer period of time, they are not eating, they are having trouble sleeping or are sleeping too much.

"You have to consider whether or not it's a pattern," says Dr. Berman. "You don't want to rush in every time your child is sad, because they're going to be sad sometimes no matter what. But if there is a dramatic loss of control or it's more frequent than is reasonable, then there's some underlying thing going on."

Many parents are uncomfortable broaching the topic of despondency. But the absolute worst choice in such a situation is ignoring the warning signs, says Dr. Berman. If parents do not feel they have adequate tools to address a bad situation, they should seek help from a professional who is familiar with adolescent depression. Aside from word-of-mouth recommendations, hospitals are probably the best source of competent mental health specialists. Call hospital public information offices for a list of reputable practitioners.

"Sometimes we act as cheerleaders when what they really need is a good ear."

Before a situation becomes this bad, however, parents can do a number of things to ease the trauma that surrounds their adolescent, says Dr. Berman. Ideally, the parent will learn to be a good listener. "You have to reassure them that there are adults around who can be trusted and who can respond with a supportive, caring, intelligent attitude, rather than simply feeding a child pablum verbally when something's going bad. You need to say, 'There are two of us dealing with this right now, not just you.' And that makes a big difference."

Parents Can Teach Coping Skills

Parents can also teach their teens coping skills, advises Dr. Berman, strategies for dealing with a range of hurts that will inevitably crop up during the teen years. Teach them how to deal with being lonely, how to manage anger and express it reasonably, how to manage anxiety. Instruction by example works well, but so does actually discussing how you, as a reasonable parent, deal with such situations yourself.

Third, parents should teach children how to use social supports when they are despondent. Young males are particularly deficient in this area. They are more often expected to deal with problems on their own and not complain about them. Teens need to know where they can go for an extra shoulder to lean on — older siblings, family members, clergy or other supportive individuals who can help when a parent is not quite what the teen is looking for.

Many times, the teen's friends are the best source of solace. So says Tamaal, a 17-year-old senior at an affluent suburban high school, who participated in a recent Gallup Institute focus group. "A friend of mine a while back was having thoughts about suicide, and he couldn't tell anyone but me. He didn't want to go to his parents because he felt they wouldn't understand. But if he wasn't able to talk to anyone, who knows what would've happened."

Parents, in turn, can also assist by not visiting their problems on their children, or not making spousal complications turn on children, Dr. Berman claims. If one adult in the household is an alcoholic, for example, the other should be responsible enough to take steps to help the rest of the family cope.

Lock Up Your Guns

One concrete action parents can take right now, today, says Dr. Berman, is to lock up any guns in the house so they are accessible only to the adults. "One of the key things that we've found over the last few years is the relationship between suicidal behavior and guns. Just having guns available to the average person means more of them are being used for suicide. That doesn't mean the gun itself is causing suicide, but it sure means that guns make it easier to act impulsively to end the pain. Put them away. Lock them up."

THE EXPERTS SUM IT UP

- Start early, say it often; reinforce anti-drug, anti-smoking, anti-drinking messages.

- Be a good example; don't smoke.

- Drink, if you do, in moderation.

- Do not leave alcohol and cigarettes lying unattended about your house.

- Be aware of long-term behavioral and attitude changes.

- Take teen depression seriously; do not brush it off.

- If you are uncomfortable discussing problems with your children, find a professional who is not.

- Teach children coping skills for being hurt, lonely and angry; how to ask for help and use social supports.

- Keep guns locked up or out of the house. Separate guns and ammunition.

- Encourage your child to develop friendships.

CHAPTER 5

The Need to Teach Values

REALITY: Too many American teens lack the one weapon with which to confront all the risks they face — solid values.

Dr. Richard Gelles, the psychiatrist and family counselor, recently faced a moment of truth in his own parenting skills with his eldest son. Accustomed to advising others, Dr. Gelles found himself running up against the very advice he offers. Why? Because he is not just a counselor. He is a parent, too. And anyone who has children understands the difference between giving good advice and yielding to it.

Dr. Gelles' son, who is 20, wanted to live and work in Los Angeles for the summer, away from his family's home in Rhode Island. Los Angeles is a big city, Dr. Gelles reasoned. It is dangerous. It is crowded. There is a great deal of violence there, much of it random. "I was afraid," he thought, "for my son to spend three months there on his own."

He hemmed and hawed. He debated using a variety of tactical maneuvers designed to thwart his son's plans. He considered issuing a peremptory "No!" He toyed with the idea of cutting off his son's funding — which would have eliminated the possibility of living in Los Angeles.

It was Dr. Gelles' younger son who pointed out that this was unjust, a form of manipulation that would do nothing but backfire on years of respectful parenting. In the end, Dr. Gelles agreed to support his son's summer plans. What was he able to rely on, despite his quite-justified concerns and fears? The very best gifts parents, and society in general, can give children: Character. Good judgment. Values. In short, the lessons every parent seeks to inculcate over the growing years until, inevitably, it is time to trust those children with what they have learned ... and let them go.

It is disheartening that the worth of good character has been downplayed in recent years, perhaps when it is needed most. As every expert we consulted insists, nothing is as essential in fighting the risks faced by our youth than a solid, early grounding in right and wrong, often rooted in religious faith. In combating drug abuse, crime, suicide, irresponsible sex, even poor health, nothing works like good character.

Passing the Torch of Values

Dr. Lickona, Professor of Education at the State University of New York and the author of several successful parenting books, thinks the slide in the importance of values started long before 1992.

"Historically, passing on a moral heritage to the young has been considered a primary responsibility of adults. That has always been the shared task of home, church and school in the past, and there has been pretty much a collaborative effort on the part of those formative institutions to pass on a legacy of values to the next generation," says Dr. Lickona, author of the 1991 parenting manual, "Educating for Character."

"That broke down in the middle of this century for a whole range of reasons," he continues. "Families came apart at the seams, the divorce rate quadrupled, adults began thinking of their own self-fulfillment as a higher obligation than the welfare of their children, and kids suffered enormously from broken homes.

"At the same time the

> *"Every problem that afflicts teen-agers today... has as a common core the absence of solid, clear values."*

families were dropping the ball, other things were fading from the lives of youngsters as moral influences. Lots of kids haven't seen the inside of a church, temple or mosque; and schools were backing away from trying to teach character because of the notion that this is a private matter and couldn't be translated authoritatively outside of the home."

Into the subsequent vacuum rushed the worst of influences — peer pressure, materialism, and television and movie violence. "Every problem that afflicts teen-agers today," says Dr. Lickona, "— violence, drug abuse, teen-age pregnancy — has as a common core the absence of solid, clear values."

Perhaps what is most surprising about this state of affairs is that teens overwhelmingly support values instruction. They say they want to be taught right from wrong. They wholeheartedly back instruction in such values as honesty and kindness. They are interested in their parents' answers to such questions as, Does God exist? and Why are we here? They believe almost to a teen in some higher authority, but want clarification on how that authority influences their daily lives.

The survey findings compiled by The Gallup International Institute provide compelling testimony for the philosophy that values need to be taught, explained, reinforced, and taught again. For the sake of clarity, we break down our findings here into three sections: How your children's schools can become involved, how you can approach the idea of spirituality in an increasingly secular society, and, finally, how parenting itself can provide the very best moral model of all.

Teach Me, Please

Teens overwhelmingly support the idea of values instruction in the classroom. The evidence? A recent Gallup Youth Survey shows a whopping 96% of teens believe lessons in honesty should be part of their regular curriculum. Another 92% feel that the curriculum should include lessons in caring for family members and friends.

Some 88% support instruction in moral courage; 85% support instruction in patriotism; 84% support instruction in the meaning of democracy; and 77% support instruction in the Golden Rule of "Do Unto Others."

Nine teens in ten, or 92%, believe schools should teach tolerance for different races, ethnicities and cultural beliefs. Some 84% of teens believe schools should teach students about various religions as a means of promoting tolerance. And though the numbers are lower, a solid majority of 57% believe tolerance for sexual orientation should be taught in the classroom (43% of teens disagree).

There is a noteworthy gender gap in these statistics. Overall young women are more supportive of the idea of tolerance instruction than are young men, by a rate of 97% to 88%. The biggest gap comes in the area of tolerance for sexual orientation. Here, 64% of young women feel tolerance for homosexuality should be taught, but slightly less than a majority of young men, or 49%, agree with them.

Still, the support is overwhelming among teens and among those experts directly involved with the fallout of their problems. So how does a school get involved in values education?

One Group's Proposition

One expert who helps school districts weave values into the curriculum is Sanford McDonnell, Chairman of the National Character Education Partnership. Based in Alexandria, Virginia, the Partnership is one of the country's largest values instruction proponents. Like other programs of character education available to schools, the Partnership's purpose, says Mr. McDonnell, retired chairman of McDonnell Douglas and a former president of the National Council of Boy Scouts, is simply to "help people get started" in character education programs.

Often, the first hurdle is convincing communities that such programs are not only useful but necessary. In his lectures across the country, Mr. McDonnell puts it simply, "When you stop and think about it, the schools have your kids for 12 and 13 years, and thousands and thousands of hours. There's no way they can avoid transmitting values. So it's not a matter of are you going to have character education, but are you going to do it in a haphazard, slipshod fashion or in a systematic, responsible way?"

To accommodate responsible action, Mr. McDonnell outlines a few basic steps. The first, most vital, step is to form a district committee comprising educators, parents and interested community residents. The question most often responsible for derailing values programs is, Whose values do you teach? Any committee that hopes for success would be charged with reaching unanimity on the character values its curriculum will teach.

"The teachers and the parents have to have ownership of the program for this to work. When you go through this committee process, you don't get any criticism of the values chosen because everyone who is concerned or interested has had a part," says Mr. McDonnell.

60% of public school teens support prayer in their schools.

"If the committee members don't agree on a specific value, it doesn't make the list.

"One of our original seven districts where we tried this values education program, for example, only came up with about six values initially. Another one came up with 30."

Honesty, responsibility and respect are the three values that make everyone's list, Mr. McDonnell adds. Other regulars across the nation include persistence, kindness, hard work, self-reliance, trustworthiness, civic virtue and fairness.

Countless Ways to Teach Values

The second step includes actually teaching the values. The ways to do this are limited only by district personnel's imaginations. Some schools, for instance, have a character trait of the month, with posters in the halls and teachers wearing buttons. Others have students write essays on given themes in their English classes. Another method, as worthy as it is timeworn, is values education through literature and storytelling. The literature in any district's curriculum is riddled with moral stories and situations that a sensitive teacher can highlight easily in the classroom.

There is also the practice of turning certain kinds of school discipline over to students, which teaches a sense of justice. Some schools require student participation on disciplinary boards; some stage debates or juries when punitive measures are necessary. "If you create a democratic classroom environment with the kids involved in the decision-making and responsibility, that's the enforcement of those very rules you are seeking to teach," says Mr. McDonnell.

Teacher training is also a crucial step in the process. Mr. McDonnell places it farther down the list of steps simply because it takes an investment in time and money that may not be readily available. It is better to get a program started, he says, and train teachers along the way. Some teachers inherently have the skills to transmit values, or know how to draw them out through classroom discussions and situations that arise naturally in the schools. Those teachers who might need additional skills can — and will — accumulate them over time.

TEENS SUPPORT EDUCATION ON TOLERANCE...	
For different races	10%
For various religions	26%
For sexual orientation	49%

Finally, Mr. McDonnell warns against insisting on lessons that, in the past, have swamped values education projects even before they get started. "For example, teaching abstinence in the context of teen sexuality is something that you cannot be in the position of telling people from the top down that they're going to have to teach. It's so volatile an issue that it can just wreck the whole program.

"My feeling is that you've just got to get started. There's

so much that can be accomplished just from teaching basic honesty and responsibility that you don't have to push that other side of it, and possibly threaten the entire project."

Mr. McDonnell adds that values should not be politicized. Lessons on right and wrong transcend the sub-issues of what to teach about AIDS and what pronouncements to make on homosexuality, single motherhood or other alternate lifestyles. What Mr. McDonnell has in mind are the very values that have been passed down from ancient civilizations. If truth, beauty, justice and wisdom were appropriate studies for ancient Greece, he says, they are just as pertinent today.

"There is no way that schools can avoid transmitting values. Are they going to do it in a systematic, responsible way?"

Just one example of organizations able to help promote values curricula, The Character Education Partnership has a full-blown community assistance program, with literature available for the asking. Partnership members are also available for consultation on how values education programs can be started in your district. Other programs are available from a variety of sources.

Spirituality in Your Home

Is religious feeling in decline in the late 20th century? Not according to the Gallup Youth Survey.

Recent polls show 95% of all teens believe in God. Of those, 76% believe in a God that participates actively in one's life, meting out rewards and punishments. Another 67% of teens believe in life after death. A full 91% of all teens believe in heaven. A considerably lower but still substantial percentage of teens, 76%, believe in hell.

Despite the overwhelming belief in some form of the divine, enough doubt is expressed in Gallup Youth Surveys to suggest that teens have not explored these questions deeply enough to satisfy their intellects or their faith.

Sixty-four percent say they are greatly interested in discussing whether there really is a God; 55%, how to decide what is right and wrong in life; 50%, why there is so much evil and hatred in the world.

Perhaps most important, 83% of teens say they long to discuss these questions with their peers, and 78% wish their parents would broach such topics.

These survey findings actually provide the basis for an opportunity. Questions and doubts — which teens have in abundance — are to be lauded and nurtured. But teens also need answers. And this is one area in which values instruction from both parents and religious institutions is invaluable. The Rev. Michael Livingston, Chaplain at the Princeton Theological Seminary, believes a solid spiritual grounding — defined primarily by each family — is an essential part of any teenager's life education.

"I would define spiritual values as those having to do with the ultimate questions of life: Who we are, how we got here, what the meaning and purpose of life is, how we are related to the source of life or the creator of life, whatever that conception is for you. And I think the search for answers to these questions is fundamental.

"Almost nothing else, in the way of instruction, will be effective if there isn't some solid foundation in spiritual values," the Rev. Livingston continues. "They are a steadying influence, a source of strength, a reference point from which a young person moves out into the world and then is able to deal with anything."

If there is spiritual confusion, the Rev. Livingston contends, there is more vulnerability to the very influences that "blow a kid off course" — drugs, peer pressures, pressures about sexuality, crime and violence. Yet while teens and children are certainly not alone in this kind of vulnerability, they are perhaps more open to spiritual answers, or at least to the pursuit of those answers.

Construct a Spiritual Household

The Rev. Livingston believes several factors are central to the construction of a spiritual household. They are qualities and characteristics, he stresses, that could be present in a variety of forms from family to family.

TEENS BELIEVE...	
In God or the divine	95%
God participates in their lives	76%
In life after death	67%
In heaven	91%
In hell	76%

For starters, there ought to be some communal aspect to the family's spiritual dimension. Spirituality is not always something that is entirely individual; instead, it has a connection to a larger community and represents one's connection to all life. Traditionally, churches, synagogues and other places of worship have fulfilled this need by providing a community of like-minded individuals.

In addition, there should be some provision in each family for reflection, for "developing an ability to listen at a very deep level to one's own spirit and perhaps to something like the divine speaking to us," says the Rev. Livingston. Today, it is not just adults that have harried lives. Teens do, as well. Their schedules are crowded with school, extracurricular activities, homework, social engagements, and in many cases, after-school jobs. Time must be set aside for their personal reflection and silence, for thinking through what one believes.

The family members themselves need to show some level of spiritual commitment. Parents should not simply take their children to Sunday school, but should attend church with them. They can learn to take advantage of

> *"Parents ought not to let their own spiritual frustration get in the way of their children's pursuit of answers."*

opportunities for discussion with their children. Recently, for example, the issue of school prayer has been getting attention in national headlines. Parents can use this as an opening to ask their children how they feel about this, or any such issue that arises spontaneously in daily life.

And for those parents whose spirituality is a source of confusion, as it is for so many, the opportunities are there to extend the search for questions to your children. Make them a part of your spiritual quest. At the very least, the Rev. Livingston says, parents ought not to let their own spiritual frustration get in the way of their children's pursuit of answers. In short, provide opportunities for children to learn about their own spirituality — independent, if need be, of your own.

Finally, parents should be open to the fact that spirituality doesn't merely involve a trip to the synagogue on Friday evening, or a Sunday morning drive to church.

"There is a more narrow approach that suggests that some things are out of the realm of spirituality, such as a walk in the woods," says the Rev. Livingston. "I believe our whole existence, everything that we experience is suffused with a sense of the divine. Not trying to limit spirituality, simply because it isn't Sunday or we're not at the synagogue, is one of the best ways to experience it throughout our lives."

Gallup surveys among adults consistently find that most Americans believe in a personal God, reachable by prayer, who judges and rewards us. Many of these people would maintain that a solid religious faith is an anchor for values and a vital foundation for young people as they face the challenges of life.

Pressing Questions for Teens

Where do teens look for answers to their pressing questions? Despite reports that they are interested only in who is going out with whom and what's on television, teens do want answers to their hard questions. And the place most children look first for answers is the home.

"When my father would try to teach me a lesson, I listened because he was the same person who fixed my bike and went fishing with me."

In his 1983 book *Raising Good Children*, Dr. Thomas Lickona, the SUNY Professor of Education, listed Ten Big Ideas parents need to understand and practice in order to transmit values. They are:

1) The core of morality is a respect for self, others and the environment that sustains all life.
2) Children develop morality slowly and in stages.
3) Respect children and require respect in return.
4) Teach children by example.

5) Teach directly by explanation and exhortation.
6) Help children learn to think, to use their own moral reasoning.
7) Help children take on real responsibilities.
8) Balance independence and control, or the child's desire for independence with the parent's need to exercise authority.
9) Love children and develop the kind of relationship that maximizes a parent's moral influence.
10) The things you do to strengthen and develop your family are the things that are going to teach them character values.

Probably most important in implementing any or all of these goals, says Dr. Lickona, is having a good relationship with one's children. "I always recommend that parents develop a close, loving relationship with their child, and then use that relationship to teach a clear sense of right and wrong. The relationship has got to be the basis, because you can't teach values to somebody you don't have a relationship with.

"When my father would try to teach me a lesson or discipline me," he adds, "I listened because he was the same person who fixed my bike and went fishing with me and played catch with me. Kids care about our values because they care about us and know that they are important to us."

Family Meetings and Chats

Dr. Lickona also supports the idea of family meetings on a weekly or at least a monthly basis. During those meetings, parents can sit down with their children and seek solutions to some simple but potentially volatile situations: How can we make bedtime easier? What can we do to make this a happier week? How can we divide the chores on Saturday?

In his own family, Dr. Lickona also made great use of "Dear Abby" newspaper columns. His family enjoyed taking turns reading the columns, and then offering their own version of advice in response. Family members not only enjoy the role-playing, but have an opportunity to clarify their values and hear how others whose opinions they respect might respond.

While many parents realize the importance of discussing life's events with their children as a means of developing character, they may not know how to go about this. Dr. Lickona offers a couple of practical solutions. One, stage a regular Q&A session with your child, for example when you're driving them home from soccer practice. Have them ask you what happened at work this week; ask them which teachers are their favorites and why, and so on. Formulate questions that cannot be answered with a simple "yes" or "no."

Parents can also make use of the "Ask Don't Tell" method of reasoning. Instead of yelling or issuing an order, force children to reason through a potentially bad situation themselves. Rather than yell at them to stop arguing over the television channel, ask them, What will happen if you continue arguing about that station? Rather than demanding that they get off the couch, ask them, What will happen if you continue to jump on that couch? The answer and the obvious action required in these cases come from the child — a far more effective way of passing along lessons in responsibility.

"Even in the difficult teen years, the parent can remain the primary reference point," says Dr. Lickona. "If there is a relationship of love and respect and the parent has built up discipline during the child's formative years, then the kids — though they may fuss about curfews and not being allowed to see R-rated movies — pretty much stay within those boundaries."

THE EXPERTS SUM IT UP

- Participate in a district-wide study of values curriculum. If one is not being planned, talk with leaders in the district about getting one started.

- The important thing in a school district is to get a values curriculum in place; don't allow it to be swamped by too-controversial "values."

- Work toward the list of core values that everyone can agree on.

- Use literature in your own home to demonstrate character and values.

- Involve your children in a community of worship.

- Set aside time in the home for reflection and silence.

- Participate in worship; don't simply drop your children off at church or synagogue.

- Develop a close, loving relationship with your children and use it to pass along values.

- Use the "Ask Don't Tell" method of reasoning.

- Encourage your children to put God first in their lives.

Meet The Experts

The Gallup International Institute gratefully acknowledges the time and thoughtfulness of these experts who shared with us their views on how parents, teachers and others who care about young people can help them avoid the risks of daily living. Their affiliations are listed below for identification purposes only, and the views expressed by these individuals do not necessarily reflect the positions of their organizations.

Dr. Lanny Berman, Director
National Center for the Study
and Prevention of Suicide
Washington School of Psychiatry
1610 New Hampshire Avenue, NW
Washington, D.C. 20009

Mr. Ross M. Burkhardt
President-Elect
National Middle School Association
c/o Shoreham-Wading River
Middle School, Randall Road
Shoreham, New York 11786

Dr. Richard Gelles, Director
Family Violence Research Program
University of Rhode Island
509A Chapee Social Science Center
Kingston, Rhode Island 02881

Ms. Tijuana James-Traore, Director
"First Things First" Program
Planned Parenthood Federation
of America
810 Seventh Avenue
New York, New York 10019

Dr. C. Everett Koop
National Safe Kids Campaign
111 Michigan Avenue, NW
Washington, D.C. 20010

Dr. Alan Leshner, Director
National Institute on Drug Abuse
5600 Fishers Lane, Room 1005
Rockville, Maryland 20857

Dr. Thomas Likona
Professor of Education
State University of New York,
Cortland
Cortland, New York 13045

Rev. Michael Livingston,
Chaplain
Princeton Theological Seminary
64 Mercer Street
Princeton, New Jersey 08542

Dr. Robert McAfee, President
American Medical Association
515 North State Street
Chicago, Illinois 60610

Mr. Sanford McDonnell, Chairman
The Character Education Partnership
c/o McDonnell Douglas
P.O. Box 516
St. Louis, Missouri 63116-0516

Mr. Thomas McMillen, Co-chair
President's Council on
Physical Fitness and Sports
701 Pennsylvania Avenue, NW
Suite 250
Washington, D.C. 20004

Ms. Trish Moylan-Torruella
Vice President for Education
Planned Parenthood Federation
of America
810 Seventh Avenue
New York, New York 10019

Dr. Cheryl Perry
Professor of Epidemiology
University of Minnesota
Grantee for: National Institute of
Alcohol Abuse and Addiction
Wilco Building, Suite 400
6000 Executive Building
Rockville, Maryland 20852

Ms. Kathryn Whitfill, President
National Parent-Teachers
Association
330 N. Wabash Avenue, Suite 2100
Chicago, Illinois 60611-3690

Mr. Kenneth Wooden, Author
The Child Lures Family Guide
Wooden Publishing House
2998 Shelburne Road
Shelburne, Vermont 05482

Resources For Parents, Teachers And Others Who Care

FROM THE GALLUP INTERNATIONAL INSTITUTE

47 Hulfish Street, Princeton, New Jersey 08542
Tel. 609-921-6200 Fax. 609-924-0228

YOUTHviews — the newsletter of The Gallup Youth Survey. Published ten times a year, *YOUTHviews* reports the findings from surveys among young people ages 13 through 17. Cost $38/year.

America's Youth in the 1990s. A compilation of Gallup Youth Surveys from 1989-1993. Cost $79.

The Religious Life of Young Americans. A compilation of Gallup Youth Surveys on young people's views on religion and values. Cost $35.

Teen Suicide. A 1994 survey among teens on their experiences with friends and others, what they see as factors that might lead to suicide, and where they go for help. Cost $29.

CRISIS HOTLINES

National Council on
Child Abuse & Family Violence 800-222-2000
CHILDHELP USA Child Abuse Hotline 800-422-4453
National Resource Center
for Child Abuse and Neglect 800-227-5242
Children's Defense Fund Crisis Hotline 800-233-1200
Covenant House Nineline 800-999-9999
National Runaway Hotline 800-231-6946
National Runaway Switchboard 800-621-4000

National Youth Crisis Hotline 800-448-4663

National Youth Suicide Hotline 800-621-4000

National Center for Missing
and Exploited Children 800-843-5678

HEALTH, EDUCATION AND
YOUTH ADVOCACY ORGANIZATIONS

National Drug Hotline
(treatment and referrals) 800-662-4357

American Council for Drug Education 800-488-3784

Just Say No International 800-258-2766

Cocaine Helpline 800-262-2463

National Council on Alcoholism
and Drug Dependence 800-622-2255

Al-Anon Family Group Headquarters 800-356-9996

National Health Information Center 800-336-4797

National Clearinghouse on Family Support
and Children's Mental Health Services 800-628-1696

National AIDS Information Clearinghouse 800-458-5231

GED Hotline 800-626-9433

National Literacy Hotline 800-228-8813

National Network of
Children's Advocacy Centers 202-639-0596

National Association of Child Advocates 202-828-6950

Resources Recommended By The Experts Consulted For This Book

Dr. Lanny Berman

National Center for the Study and Prevention of Suicide.

Adolescent Suicide: Assessment and Intervention. 1991, co-authored with David Jobes. American Psychological Association publication written for clinicians but can be read and understood by laypersons.

Mr. Ross Burkhardt

National Middle School Association.

These publications, oriented toward parents, can be ordered over the phone with VISA/MASTERCARD from the Association, 2600 Corporate Exchange Drive, Suite 370, Columbus, Ohio 43231. Tel. 614-895-4730.

"H.E.L.P. — How to enjoy living with a pre-adolescent." Pamphlet, free for one copy, bundles of 50 @ $15.

"More H.E.L.P." Pamphlet. Cost the same as above.

Grounded for Life: Stop blowing your fuse and start communicating with your teenager. Book, $17/copy.

Dr. Alan Leshner

National Institute on Drug Abuse

The Institute has a major public information program with pamphlets and brochures available free to the public through the National Clearinghouse for Alcohol and Drug Information, at 1-800-729-6686. Examples of pamphlets include the free "A Parent's Guide to Prevention: Growing Up Drug-Free," and "Tips for Teens," a series of six pamphlets detailing six controlled substances. This 800 number also serves as a general information line for parents who are concerned that their teens are abusing drugs or alcohol and who need a description of symptoms; the clearinghouse will fax or send out a fact sheet based on parents' concerns. However, it is not a counseling service.

Dr. Thomas Lickona

Author and Professor of Education, SUNY

Educating for Character, 1991, Bantam Books. How to instill character and values in the lives of your children.

Raising Good Children, 1993, Bantam Books. Includes details on Dr. Lickona's ten big ideas on which parents should focus in raising children of good character.

Sex, Love and You: Making the Right Decision, 1994, Ave Maria Press, co-authored with Judy Lickona and William Boudreau, M.D. Guide for teens on sexual abstinence.

Dr. Robert McAfee
American Medical Association

The "AMA's Gaps" program discussed in this book is an acronym for "The American Medical Association's Guidelines for Adolescent Preventive Services." The pamphlet is available to the public at $24 for AMA members and $29.95 for non-members. The pamphlet can be ordered directly from the AMA via VISA/MASTERCARD. The American Medical Association, 515 North State Street, Chicago, Illinois 60610. Tel. 312-464-5000. For pamphlet orders, 1-800-621-8335.

Mr. Sanford McDonnell
The Character Education Partnership

This is one of the nation's largest organizations involved with values and character education in the schools. Call directly for the latest catalog, which lists books, pamphlets, videos, audiotapes and curriculum guides, some free, some for a fee, available to the public. The Partnership also provides different levels of consultants who visit communities and schools and provide lectures on coordinating a values development project. The Character Education Partnership, c/o Association for Supervision and Curriculum Development, 1250 North Pitt Street, Alexandria, Virginia 22314-1453. Tel. 703-739-9515.

Mr. Thomas McMillen
President's Council on Physical Fitness and Sports

Various free pamphlets, available by calling the Council directly, include "Running," "Fitness Fundamentals,"(describing a sports award program) and "Kids in Action" (for ages 2-17 showing exercises children and teens should do). Available from the Council, 701 Pennsylvania Avenue NW, Suite 250, Washington, D.C. 20004. Tel. 202-272-3421.

Ms. Trish Moylan-Torrula
Planned Parenthood Federation of America

The Federation has a network of 600 sexuality educators, many focused on the prevention of bH.I.V./AIDS and safe sex. The Federation has local affiliates in 49 states, available for community or classroom consultation. For the nearest affiliate, call 1-800-230-PLAN.

Some brochures (free for single copies; fee for multiple copies) available by contacting a local affiliate are, "What Kids Should Learn and When They Should Learn It" and "Teens and AIDS."

Mr. Kenneth Wooden
Wooden Publishing House

The Child Lures Family Guide, 1994. Cost $4. Order directly from Wooden Publishing House, 2998 Shelburne Road, Shelburne, Vermont 05482. The author interviewed over 1,000 individuals involved with or convicted of such crimes as kidnapping, molestation, rape and murder to develop a list of the types of "universal lures" perpetrators use to trap their victims.

OTHER RESOURCES

VIOLENCE PREVENTION

Kids and Violence, 1994, edited by Linda McCart. 42 pages. $15. National Governors' Association, 444 North Capitol Street, Washington, D.C. 20001-1512. Tel. 202-624-5300. This report includes an annotated resource list of the most recent publications on youth violence, including a guide to organizations that provide information and technical assistance.

The Prevention of Youth Violence: A Framework for Community Action. National Center for Injury Prevention and Control, Centers for Disease Control and Prevention, 4770 Buford Highway NE, Mail Stop F36, Atlanta, Georgia 30341. Tel. 404-448-4690. This publication provides information for locating resources from private and public agencies. It also lists useful reading materials and effective local programs from around the country.

Deadly Consequences: How Violence is Destroying Our Teenage Population and a Plan to Begin Solving the Problem, 1991, Deborah Prothrow-Stith, M.D. with Michael Weissman. 269 pages. $12. Harper Collins Publisher, PO Box 588, Dunmore, Pennsylvania 18512. Tel. 800-331-3761. The appendix lists organizations state-by-state that conduct violence prevention and intervention programs.

Preventing Violence: Program Ideas and Examples, 1992. 76 pages. Free. National Crime Prevention Council, 1700 K Street, NW, Second Floor, Washington, D.C. 20006-3817. Tel. 202-466-6272. Describes violence prevention programs from around the country. A resource guide is also included.

Parent's Checklist

Which of these applies to you? Grade yourself in parenting skills.

Do you try hard always to. . .

Live an ethical and moral life yourself?	+3
Develop a close, loving relationship with your children?	+3
Spend "quantity" time as well as "quality" time with your child?	+3
Make it easy for your children to share inner needs, hurts and hopes with you?	+3
Stay alert to long-term behavioral and attitude change, or periods of despondency?	+3
Be receptive to seeking outside help if and when a situation seems unmanageable?	+3
Know your child's friends?	+3
Make sure you know where your children are going when they are going "out" or to a party?	+3

Have you. . .

Told your child *today* that you loved him or her?	+3
Asked your child *this week* whether his or her life at school was better than O.K.? (If the answer was "no" did you make it easy for your child to tell you why it was not?)	+3
Had a discussion *this month* with your child about the rightness or wrongness of a situation?	+3

Supported a values curriculum in your school or talked with others about starting one?	+3
Ever talked with your child about the meaning of life, values, or religion?	+3
Made sure you teen has access to confidential health-care counseling?	+3
Had a frank discussion on sex, sharing your own philosophy or beliefs (appropriate to the age of the child)?	+3

Does your child's teacher. . .

Know how to reach you during the day and at home?	+3
Know that you want to hear when your child is doing well and not so well?	+3

Do you. . .

Permit violence in your home by striking out at others, by your language, by accepting violence or laughing at it?	-3
Have a loaded gun in your home in a place where a child might gain access to it?	-3
Allow your children to watch whatever TV they want, whenever they want?	-3

Your Score:_____

How Are You Doing?

40 to 51	Super parent. Keep up the good work!
30 to 39	You're giving your children good support, but you can do better. Look over the quiz for ideas.
20 to 29	Your child needs more of your help. Look over the questions again and see how you can help them more. Perhaps talk with friends or with your minister, rabbi or other spiritual leader for guidance.
Less than 20	Your child may feel that he or she cannot turn to you for help. Perhaps professional guidance can help you and your family. Take along this quiz and your answers. Listen to the advice you receive and act on it. Your child needs your support and help.